40 Common Errors
IN GOLF
and How to Correct Them

Author-photographer Art Shay (left) "instructs" Jack Nicklaus (right) and a Time magazine reporter in Arnold Palmer's method of holding the putter.

Some 15 years after instructing Nicklaus, Shay "instructs" Oak Park Country Club pro Ray Williams, who posed for some of the pictures in this book.

40 Common Errors
IN GOLF
and How to Correct Them

Arthur Shay

CONTEMPORARY
BOOKS, INC.
CHICAGO

Library of Congress Cataloging in Publication Data

Shay, Arthur.
  40 common errors in golf and how to correct them.

  Includes index.
  1. Golf.   I. Title.
GV965.S498   1978   796.352'3   77-23706
ISBN 0-8092-7828-6
ISBN 0-8092-7827-8 pbk.

Published by Contemporary Books, Inc.
180 North Michigan Avenue, Chicago, Illinois 60601
Manufactured in the United States of America
Library of Congress Catalog Card Number: 77-23706
International Standard Book Number: 0-8092-7828-6 (cloth)
                                    0-8092-7827-8 (paper)

Published simultaneously in Canada by
Beaverbooks, Ltd.
150 Lesmill Road
Don Mills, Ontario M3B 2T5
Canada

Contents

Acknowledgments

I would like to thank the following professional golfers and instructors, mostly PGA members, for their help in the preparation of this book: Ray Williams, Oak Park Country Club, Elmwood Park, Illinois, and his assistants, Tim Stare, Dick Horsting, and Ron Goodman; Jack Webb, Wakonda Golf Club, Des Moines, Iowa (on cover); Bruce Wood, Tippecanoe Lake Country Club, Tippecanoe, Indiana; Steve Goering, Exmoor Country Club, Highland Park, Illinois; Victor Regalado, Tijuana Country Club, Mexico; Andy Bean, Champion Country Club, Houston, Texas; Sam Adams, Boone, North Carolina; Bobby Stroble, Metropolitan Golf Course, Albany, Georgia; Steve Dunning, Golf, Illinois; Chi Chi Rodriguez, Rio Mar Country Club, Puerto Rico; Jack Nicklaus (*Time* magazine photo); Gary Wintz, The Club at Indigo, Daytona Beach, Florida; Don Iverson, La Crosse Country Club, La Crosse, Wisconsin; Lee Elder, Washington, D.C.; Arnold Palmer, the first "master" I ever photographed; Dave Ogilvie, Flossmoor Country Club, Flossmoor, Illinois.

Special thanks to chief pro Earl Puckett for permitting me to photograph Ray Williams on the beautiful Oak Park Country Club course, the Butler National Golf Club, Oakbrook, Illinois, and the PGA officials of the Western Open.

this "gutty" ball launched the sport from Scotland to the rest of the world. The "gutty" was easier to hit, flew farther, and lasted longer. By the turn of the century there were a quarter-million American golfers. Rubber bands at the core of the gutta-percha ball helped the game develop. The liquid-center ball arrived in 1899. Today there are some twenty million golfers, around ten thousand golf courses, and some seven thousand teaching professionals in the United States alone.

At the time I worked with Wind. I had had but one startling golf experience. The very first time I drove a golf ball, at a range near Armonk, New York, I stunned a racing rabbit about sixty yards downfield. My accuracy has steadily gone downhill since then, but not my interest in golf or my admiration for its masters.

The first "master" I met was Arnold Palmer. It was in the early sixties in Denver, right after the U.S. Open. I had been hired by Munsingwear to photograph Palmer, Jackie Burke, Dow Finsterwald, and one or two others in Munsingwear shirts. The Chicago ad man who arranged for the photograph put us all up in his large suite at the Brown Palace Hotel.

The morning after I shot the ad we were having breakfast in the coffee shop. I mentioned to the pros that *Life* magazine's sports editor, Jack McDermott, had said *Life* would welcome a good golf story if I could come up with one. I put the problem on the table as we waited for our eggs.

"If I showed you a bunch of contact prints taken during a tournament," I said to the pros, "could you look at the pictures and tell me what you were thinking or feeling at the time?" "Hey," Palmer said, "that's a great idea...."

Thus, at the next Master's Tournament in Augusta, I covered Palmer for four days, photographing just about every-

thing he did. He played well, and the excitement of golf had me forever in its grip. On the final day, Palmer, followed by his "army," birdied the seventeenth and eighteenth holes to win. Palmer's own words ran with the pictures. My resolve to use words and pictures in a golf book began at that time. My approach, I decided, would be to get teaching pros to pose for, then explain the pictures.

As I've traveled around the country in my work as a writer and photographer, I've stopped at several dozen golf clubs and asked the club pro, "What common mistakes are your students making and how do you help them correct these mistakes?" As my list of mistakes and corrections got longer, and my sheaf of photographs heavier, I knew that, although I would never break 85 as a golfer, I could help golfers across the country take a stroke off their game here, another stroke off there.

Pros from California, Texas, Florida, Ohio, Illinois, and elsewhere took the time and trouble to help me. Golf pros are so used to helping people that I can't think of one who turned me down. Each took the time to provide an error and its correction.

After I had gathered a good part of my mistake-correction photos together, I sought out Ray Williams, a brilliant, young teaching pro who had abandoned the tour to teach golf at the Oak Park Country Club west of Chicago. With the help of Williams and some of his staff I sifted the mistakes and corrections down to those errors that were most common among average golfers who take lessons. When Williams thought my mistake or correction pictures didn't clearly show what was wrong or right, he served as model as we reshot the sequences. Williams found it especially difficult to assume "mistake" positions!

"Demonstrating these mistakes is go-

Introduction

Probably, humans on all continents have been striking away at makeshift balls with makeshift clubs since we came out of the trees. Writer, TV host, and a golfer who has teed off on most of the continents, Alistair Cooke has written: "To get an elementary grasp of the game of golf, a human must learn, by endless practice, a continual and subtle series of highly unnatural movements, involving about 64 muscles, that result in a seemingly 'natural' swing, taking all of two seconds to begin and end."

It was just north of Cooke's native England, in Scotland's hills, braes, lochs, and weather, that golf was invented. It developed from *paganica*, played by the occupying Romans around 200 A. D. So, golf took hold centuries ago. That American Scot, Andrew Carnegie, the benevolent steel man, called golf an "indispensable adjunct to high civilization." The resurrector of Carnegie's words happens to be the best sportswriter who ever

lived, Herbert Warren Wind, whose favorite sport is golf and who says (in his book *The Complete Golfer*) of golf: "Perhaps it is nothing more than the best game man has ever devised."

Years ago, as a *Sports Illustrated* photographer, I had the pleasure and honor of covering a golf match with Wind in Indiana. He insisted on carrying one of my camera bags with telephoto lenses; I have never had a more distinguished caddy.

As we walked the fairways on a bright summer's day, Wind told me of an extraordinary English golfer of long ago, Harry Vardon, who was so systematic in his strokes from day to day that he would make allowances in his swing so that he didn't end up in his own divots. Wind's knowledge of golf was (and is) encyclopedic. He told me of the old leather-skinned balls stuffed with feathers that the Scots had used for centuries. In 1848 the gutta-percha ball came along, and ing to kill my game," he wailed. "It's making me visualize bad shots!" He got over it by the time we were done.

Before the Western Open near Chicago, big money-winner Andy Bean let me photograph him as he practiced his putting. Chi Chi Rodriguez posed for a trick two-headed photograph joking with the gallery as usual. Lee Elder waved in remembrance of a discussion we once had in Ohio about his work in Washington, D.C., with ghetto youngsters who wanted to become golfers. Victor Regalado of Mexico said, "I won't show you no mistake before a match, amigo!" Bobby Stroble took the time to demonstrate his controversial and difficult right arm cocking motion.

Once, while photographing a much younger and much heavier Jack Nicklaus for a *Time* magazine cover story, we posed in front of his little Columbus, Ohio, house after his wife had made breakfast for my two reporters and me. Clownishly, I showed Nicklaus and the *Time* writers how Palmer had taught me to hold the putter.

After this one short lesson, Nicklaus went on to become the greatest golfer who ever lived!

I can't promise that degree of success to all those who read this book and learn how to correct some of their mistakes. All I can do is dedicate this book to some representative golfers who make at least forty typical mistakes: prominent Chicago ad man, Ira Brichta; Jack McDermott, golf enthusiast and editor of *Signature* magazine; and the vast army of golfers I can't possibly, in person, show how to hold that putter.

Arthur Shay

Chapter 1
Starting out

MISTAKE

Choosing the wrong clubs

Many young golfers inherit clubs, grow up with them, and then adapt their own body size and swing to them.

If you are starting out in golf and can afford to pick and choose, it is a mistake to make these choices lightly or on the recommendation of anyone but a good golf club "fitter" in a pro shop. It's a mistake to forget that club-making and marketing is an intensely competitive business.

Thin handles are wrong for thick-handed people. Stronger-armed golfers make a mistake in choosing a shaft that is too flexible. And the use of steel shafts as opposed to titanium, fiberglass, and now graphite is a battle constantly being fought by manufacturers and pros. Beginning golfers should not be psyched into using one kind over another.

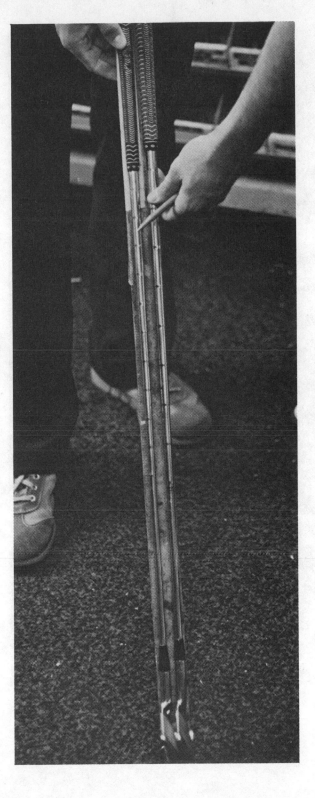

CORRECTION

After you have wandered a bit in the happy jungles of club availability and style and listened to or read the available data on the different kinds of clubs, ask your pro to measure you for clubs. Using a simple yardstick device, he or she will be able to tell you precisely what length club is best for your height and arm length. Arm length is the crucial measurement.

From here, a reputable and well-stocked pro shop will let you experiment with used clubs that are your size but have varying weights. Soon you'll get the "feel" that will serve as a starting point.

If you really take to golf, you probably will join the majority of golfers—especially the pros—who experiment with different clubs over their entire golfing lives. Putters alone fill many a pro's basement. I remember Arnold Palmer spending many an off hour during the Master's Tournament working on his clubs, altering them very slightly in weight or length, changing the grips on some, and, in subtle ways I couldn't understand, improving others.

Some male golfers do better with lighter-weight clubs designed for women, and some women play better with men's clubs. Practice, experiment—but start out with a professional measurement, as you would with a suit that costs as much as those clubs.

Basically, the taller a golfer is, the closer he can come to a classic swing because, theoretically, the ball will be closer to him when he swings and his longer arc will provide more speed than a shorter player can get. But Ben Hogan played at five-foot-three!

MISTAKE

Not warming up

Most bodies, like cars, take a little warming up to run smoothly and efficiently. Not warming up properly results in stiff swings, minimal ·accuracy, and sometimes injuries to ankles and muscles.

4

CORRECTION

The latest research in sport medicine tells us that stretching those muscles before using them in earnest prepares them for their task. The golf club makes a fine stretching aid. Bend your body to awaken those big back muscles where your power lies. Turn from side to side, holding a golf club at both ends. Knee bends and short jogs (if jogging suits your temperament) also are useful in getting your motor up to performance levels.

Chapter 2
The grip

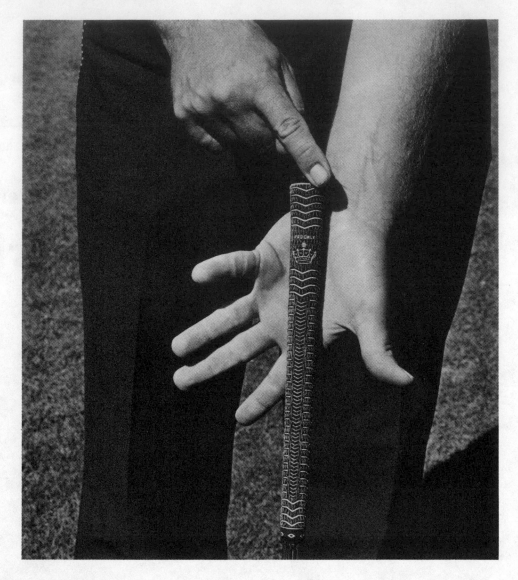

MISTAKE

Poor grip

Some golfers, even pros, use unorthodox grips. This is a mistake for the golfer who wishes to progress as quickly as possible in golf. If you feel the club shift in your hand as you make contact with the ball, if your fingers fly off the handle, if swinging the club causes you pain in the wrists or gets you knotted up in your follow-through, chances are you are using an unorthodox, poorly coordinated grip.

Most of the poor and unorthodox grip woes in golf can be traced to the *palm of the hand*. A club centered in the palm makes it difficult for the fingers to do their important job—gripping. This centering of the club handle in the palm often compounds gripping woes by causing the player to grip the club too loosely or too tightly, resulting in inaccuracy.

Vardon

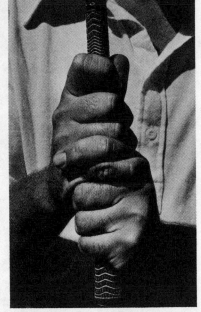

Interlocking

10-finger

CORRECTION

The first step you must take en route to choosing the grip that works best for you is to start your grip by letting the handle of the club rest at the base of your fingers—*not the center of the palm.*

Then you are ready to join the 99 percent of good golfers who use one of the three grips pictured here: the Vardon, the interlocking, and the 10-finger (baseball) grip.

The most popular is the Harry Vardon grip, in which the little finger of the right hand overlaps the index finger of the left hand. The next most popular grip is the interlocking grip, in which the little finger of the right hand interlocks with the index finger of the left hand, weaving the hands together. Jack Nicklaus uses this grip. The third is called the 10-finger or baseball grip. Bob Rosburg has won many a tournament with this grip.

If your wrists (and hands) are weak, try clenching rubber balls a few minutes a day and flexing your wrists against an invisible elastic that's trying to keep you from stretching it.

MISTAKE

Piccolo grip

For some nonchauvinistic reason, many women players begin to raise their club in the backswing correctly, then, when the club goes up over their head, the fingers of the left hand loosen into the light touch required for playing the piccolo. This collapse in the grip breeds scatter-shots and downright misses.

10

CORRECTION

A conscious effort must be made to squeeze that grip as you begin your stroke. This is true of all racquet and bat sports, too. If sheer weakness prevents a strong enough grip, then squeezing a rubber ball a few minutes a day will lend strength to the average hand. Grip control means shot control. If you learn to squeeze somewhat harder, you will gain accuracy and power—two fine golf dividends for merely getting a grip on your grip.

11

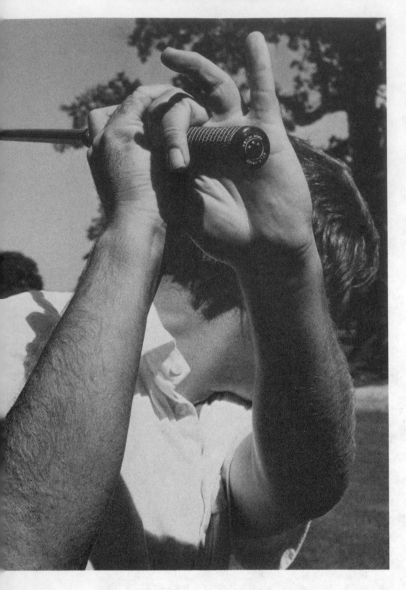

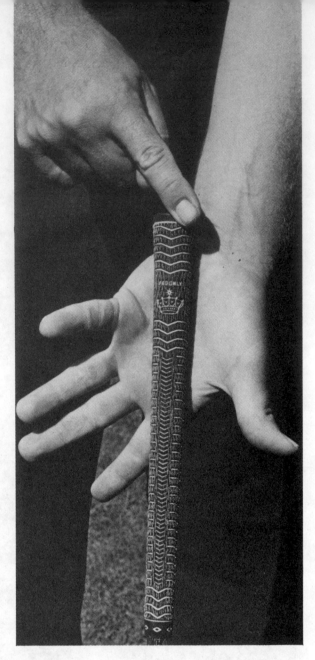

MISTAKE

Losing your grip

There are several varieties of this mistake, all bad. One of the most common occurs when the bottom two fingers of the left hand jump away from the club handle at the top of the swing.

The primary reason for this mistake occurs at the moment the player grasps the club—and places the handle *in the palm* of the left hand. By the time the swing gets overhead, the last fingers begin to lift away from the handle and loss of power and precision follows.

CORRECTION

The club must be grasped by the *fingers of the left hand*, just where the palm begins. This is absolutely crucial to the development of an effective, consistent grip. No matter which of the standard grips you employ, a good grip starts with the handle of the club at the base of the fingers—*not in the palm!*

MISTAKE

Flipping of hands

At the end of an otherwise good swing, the hands may suddenly flip, or bend, at the wrist, bringing the club skyward close to the body. A sudden loss of accuracy and distance result from flipping, as well as placing unnecessary strain on the hands and wrist. At the moment of impact in a bad swing, the back of the left hand suddenly faces the sky. During the "flip," the right hand takes over the stroke, causing the "menagerie" of errors.

14

CORRECTION

Perfecting your grip takes as much practice as perfecting other, more spectacular departments of golf. Conscious pressure and firmness must be exerted at the moment of impact to keep the hands on their "plane," their trajectory, and to keep the wrists from suddenly collapsing and giving up their important function of supporting the entire stroke.

Chapter 3

Setting up your body

MISTAKE

Stiff address

It's wrong to address the ball with the merest bend in your legs, back, and head. This stiffness will prevent a good weight shift from back leg to front leg. A golf club shaft positioned at the stiff player's waist will make a straight line along the player's back—a no no.

Too much knee bend (to make up for that straight up and down back) will result in a jerky swing.

CORRECTION

With the knees flexed just slightly, the head should bend into a comfortable position. The club shaft, used as a straight edge, now will make a smooth line from the head down the back about halfway. You can see the degree of difference in the bend required. The address should start fairly straight-legged. When you are ready to aim, just "sit down" about two or three inches, no more.

19

MISTAKE

Poor set-up

In a golfer's eagerness, he often positions the ball too far forward. The shoulders will then, during the swing, move to the left, causing a slice, the ball curving from left to right. Many mis-hits result from this common error. In the photo, a spare club has been positioned on the ground so that you can see the ball in its bad relationship to the left foot.

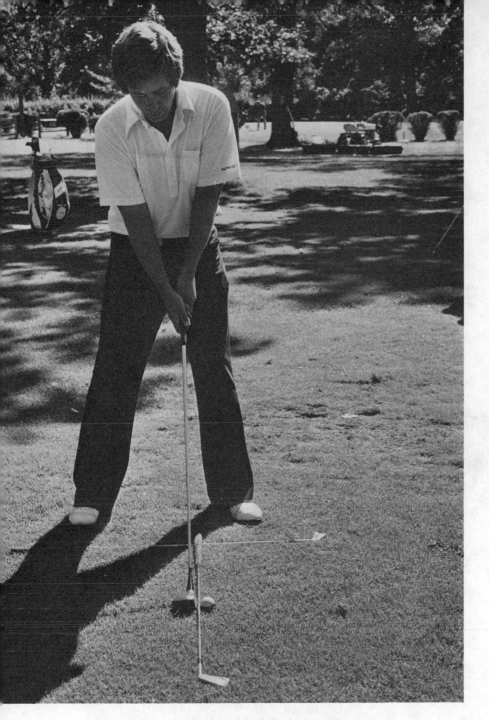

CORRECTION

With the ball moved back toward the center of the body, the shoulders now will be aimed properly at the target, and the swing will let you use your power to drive the ball, rather than loft, top, or miss it. (Don't forget to take that spare club away before you swing!)

MISTAKE

Lifting the heel

A slight lifting or rolling of the left heel is a common problem that may exist from the beginning or slip into a golfer's swing gradually. Basically, this error is responsible for what pro Ray Williams calls "the menagerie"—the entire unwelcome family of errors: inaccuracy, poor power, etc. Lifting the heel causes poor use of your body and often results in a "fat" shot, that is, hitting behind the ball.

CORRECTION

The heel is crucial in the transfer of body weight from the back foot to the front foot. As in most areas of golf, there are at least two large armies of opinion. In the case of the heel, both armies have expert leaders. Jack Nicklaus uses a slight rolling motion of the foot and lifts his heel slightly as he swings.

Gene Littler uses a slight rolling motion, but his heel doesn't lift.

You should practice both of these methods and adopt whichever one cures your "menagerie" of heel-related faults.

MISTAKE

Poor weight shift

On the longer wedge or short iron shots, usually approach shots, where some body power is required, the body's weight shifts erroneously backward. This usually contributes to the collapse of the wrists, as in the Scooping error. Consistency is sacrificed, shanking (ball is hit too close to the shaft) is risked, and the ball may be topped and flubbed.

CORRECTION

Concentrate on keeping those wrists from "breaking," that is, keep them fairly rigid. Get into the rhythm of shifting the weight from the back foot to the front one. A few preparatory waggles of the body will help you get the backward-forward rhythm. This stroke is led by the arms and wrists, and aid from the body's forward movement should be enlisted smoothly and gradually. This is one of the easiest golf shots for the beginner to learn because it is a slow-motion shot that can be "felt" when you get it down.

MISTAKE

Moving head

The head is the keystone around which the entire golf swing circles. When you lift, jerk, or otherwise move your head, you set up a terrible chain of events during a golf stroke. With head movement, the easy turn of the shoulders into the shot is restricted. A majority of bad drives go off to the right because a moving head doesn't give an adequate pivot point for a good swing.

CORRECTION

Think of the head as an axis or hub around which the swing revolves. The less it moves the better. It may take you a while to develop a comfortable chin position, and you may have to do what Jack Nicklaus does—point your chin slightly to the right as you start your swing. This slight alteration from a straight up and down head position will help you get a better pivot and more accurate swing.

MISTAKE

Head bobbing

When the head·bobs up and down, as Chi Chi Rodriguez demonstrates in a double exposure, the entire stroke is thrown off, as it is in almost any kind of exaggerated head movement. Head bobbing throws off the entire axis and rhythm of a good golf swing.

28

CORRECTION

The head must be the fulcrum around which the golf swing moves. Its movement should be absolutely minimal during the golf swing. Your head can move slightly from a rigid position, but it should move with the shoulders, not independently.

Chapter 4
The swing

MISTAKE .

Dipping

In dipping, the swing starts well, but just before impact, your head and shoulder dip down. Instead of hitting or stroking the ball, you end up swatting it erratically, hitting behind the ball or shanking it.

CORRECTION

The key to correcting dipping is to keep that left arm and right shoulder from breaking down and pulling the right shoulder and head down. Concentrate on keeping the shoulders parallel to the ground at time of impact.

MISTAKE

Poor aiming

Almost all golfers make aiming errors that result in slicing—hitting to the right when you don't want the ball to go in that direction. Some golfers incorporate slicing into their game; others break out in slices periodically.

The culprit in slicing is poor aiming—not lining up so that the ball is struck when the club head is facing the target squarely. Contributing largely, is that old bugaboo, a faulty backswing. This type of faulty backswing sends the club out and away from the body, then pulls it in at the last uncoordinated second. The club face cuts across the ball, putting a spin on it that makes the ball lurch off to the right.

This golfer is aiming, erroneously, at the big tree. Alas, he'll hit it.

CORRECTION

A slight change in foot position, moving that left foot to the left and the right foot to the right, is enough to effect a better body position for aiming right down the fairway rather than toward the trees.

Birdie Tebbetts said of baseball that it is a game of inches. So is golf. A fraction of an inch difference in where the club face strikes the ball makes yards and yards of difference in where the ball lands. This is perhaps truer in aiming than in any other department of golf.

Thus, in practice you should work on getting that club face to hit the ball at the moment it is facing the target—whether it's a green or a spot on the fairway straight ahead.

The key to curing the outside-to-inside swing, responsible for more slices than Kraft, is to make sure that at the top of your backswing your right foot is still carrying most of your body's weight. The left arm should be straight and the right elbow pointing at the ground.

Some of the difficulties in aiming and outside-in swinging come from not being able to analyze what you are doing wrong. Some pros recommend that you tee up as you would normally, then place another ball on a tee six inches to the left and six inches ahead of the "normal" ball. If you're swinging outside-in, after your target ball goes slicing off to the right, you'll also hit that second ball or come near hitting it. Practice your aiming and your backswing until you avoid the second ball.

MISTAKE

Laying the club off

"Laying the club off" is golf pro language for badly aiming the head of your club at the top of the backswing. The usual "menagerie" of troubles, notably slicing, can result from this mistake.

36

CORRECTION

Sometimes the correction of this error is as simple as cutting down the height you raise your left heel during your swing. Attention should be paid, too, to a comfortable, natural "break" of the wrists as they are taken up and back in the backswing.

It may be wise to start all over and work on a "new" backswing. Points to watch: take the club back with both hands; *don't* let the wrists turn! Billy Caspar recommends "the best way to start the swing is with a push of the left hand away from the target, making certain that the right hand exerts no influence. . . ."

37

MISTAKE

Flat-footed stance

If you lock your legs flatly onto the ground and swing as in the photo, you will not be taking advantage of most of the power available from your body. Your stroke will be all arms, wrists, and hands. You won't get any appreciable distance. Moreover, your club head will hit the ball at an angle, starting its flight to the left, but then slicing, as the majority of bad golf shots do, to the right.

CORRECTION

Foot and leg action must be altered so that the weight of the body can be shifted from the back foot to the front in a smooth motion—the ball being hit about midway through this vital shift.

The trick is to balance the body's weight on the balls of the feet, not on flat-footed soles. You must be prepared to roll your weight from back foot to front foot. At first, it feels as though your weight is on the outside of your back (right) foot, and then it moves across to the outside of your front (left) foot.

It's actually much like a dance step—a phrase that often terrifies golfers—and the phrase "don't stand there flat-footed!" is used by dance as well as golf instructors. We're talking about rhythm, and you must practice swinging rhythmically unless you were born with rhythm.

The payoff for a good, non-flat-footed swing comes in getting rid of what Ray Williams calls the "menagerie" of golf errors: poor distance, hooking, slicing, etc.

MISTAKE

Stance too wide

If you take too wide a stance as you set up to hit the ball, you are also cutting down on your body's ability to turn with your swing. You're defeating the whole purpose of the coordinated golf swing. Proper use of feet, legs, arms, torso, and shoulders is severely restricted by starting out with your legs too far apart. Generally, golfers determined to hit "real hard" widen their stance (erroneously of course) to get all the power they can muster behind their shot.

CORRECTION

In practice, when you feel the flat-footed, uncoordinated discomfort of a swing that isn't getting your body's power into the ball, try moving your feet a little closer. Vary the distance until you feel that you've got a good base for your swing. The weight of your body should rest on the balls of your feet as you take your new, narrower stance.

MISTAKE

Takeaway troubles

One of the most crucial parts of the golf swing is the first foot or so of the backswing, as the club moves away from the ball. A jerky motion here will throw off the entire swing, as will premature cocking of the wrists or any quick wrist motion. The trouble, starting this early, will compound by the time the stroke is at its height, and inaccuracy will result.

CORRECTION

For most golfers the easiest takeaway to master is the smooth takeaway shown, with the wrists beginning to break just after the first foot of backward travel by the club.

Some gifted pros, Bobby Stroble, for example, use a "one piece" takeaway, with the wrists not breaking until the arms are much higher. This is more difficult to learn, but it is a joy to watch when done right.

MISTAKE

Overswing

Beginning golfers with weak arms or faulty grips often compound their difficulties by overswinging—letting the club droop down toward the ground at the height of the backswing. This results in a loss of control over the shot to be made, and it often accounts for the embarrassment suffered by all beginners of an absolute miss. The jerky arm motion of the overswing tends to pull the chin up, adding disaster to disaster.

CORRECTION

Sometimes lighter or slightly shorter golf clubs are the answer to overswinging. Most often, however, determination is needed to hold onto that grip and to keep the left arm straight as it goes into the backswing.

Hand and arm exercises can be of some help to the young, aspiring golfer. Here again, a mental picture of where the backswing should be overhead should help to put it there at the right time. That chin should be trained to stay tucked into the shoulder, too.

45

MISTAKE

Incomplete backswing

For some reason—possibly undeveloped biceps—young golfers of both sexes, and women golfers in general, are troubled by the compulsion to end the backswing before it has "swung back."

This results in a loss of power and the chronic complaint of new golfers: "Why can't I hit the ball *farther*?"

Other backswing woes: taking the club back with the hands instead of with the shoulders and arms; head bobs; body wavers from a good, central position; ball is hit on an outside to inside angle.

46

CORRECTION

The backswing is one of those golf motions that responds to a mental visualization of what you want to do. That is, you can't see the club laid out parallel to the ground because it's over your head. But from the start of the backswing, you can imagine the way it should go and try to make it happen with the muscles you have available to you. "Muscle memory," the physiologists call it.

Practice a good shoulder turn, with a slight, gentle hip movement toward the ball. Wrists should be fairly rigid as you move the club back from the ball, left arm straight. Remember where you want the club during its momentary overhead position and get it there, keeping your chin well down. A gentle flexing of the knees as you swing completes the backswing. Now all you have to do is hit the ball well!

MISTAKE

Improper shoulder turn

Failing to turn your shoulders far enough to the right when you swing is responsible for improper weight distribution at the moment of contact with the ball. Inconsistency will develop in the swing, and inaccuracy will result if this mistake is not corrected. If the head of the club is not facing the target area at the top of your backswing, your shoulder turn is the culprit. If the club head is pointing in any direction other than the target, the ball's inaccuracy will increase. Slices, hooks, and worse come from poor shoulder turning. The worst shoulder turns occur when your hands, arms, and shoulders do not work as a unit—but the shoulders usually are the main problem.

48

CORRECTION

The correction for the bad habit of poor shoulder turning begins, very gently, with the hips. To keep the shoulders and upper part of the body behind the ball, a slight push outward of the left hip will help some players. Mentally, it helps to think of a good turn as one that help you swing right through the ball and on up into the follow-through. A proper turn can be felt, and you can practice it without hitting a ball—just swinging and feeling the transfer of weight from back to front foot as you do it right.

The shoulders should lead the action of the hands, arms, and shoulders, but somehow hands, arms, and shoulders must work together for a perfect turn. Try slowing down the shoulders as they start this shot. The grip of the left hand at the top of the backswing should be slightly stronger than that of the right hand—firm but not vise-tight.

49

MISTAKE

Getting ahead of the ball

When the head and shoulders move ahead of the ball during the swing, there is a tendency to "top" the shot, hit it very low on the face of the club, or miss the ball completely. Generally, the shot goes low and slices off to the right with minimal power.

Note that the golfer's head is lined up with the tree behind him as he starts the swing. By midswing, you can see how far he has gotten ahead of the ball by comparing the vertical line of the tree. (He wasn't trying to hit the ball for this illustration.)

CORRECTION

The golfer must concentrate on keeping his or her head relatively still. The shoulders must be made to move in a pivot, rather than in a lunging or forward motion. The head is, of course, the pivotal "center post" in a good golf swing. It helps some golfers to keep their left shoulder level with the ground during the swing, which keeps it from dipping and thrusting the body forward.

MISTAKE

Swatting

As a golfer gets older, he or she tends to swat at the ball rather than hit it. Golfers begin to depend more on their arms and hands than on their bodies. This diminishes distance quite a bit, but sometimes it helps older golfers maintain and even improve their accuracy. (I once did a *Sports Illustrated* story on a 90-year-old golfer who "shot his age"!)

Sometimes the "stiffness" of those big back and leg muscles that provide most of the power for golf swings is based on a medical condition. In that case, swat away as best you can. But if you are generally limber—say, limber enough to walk through a round of golf—swatting may be a correctable mistake.

CORRECTION

If you are swatting the ball and feel that you are physically capable of getting more of your body into your swing than just arms and wrists, try a few of the stretching exercises shown on page 5 before starting your round. Stretching those large back and waist muscles as you hold a golf club at both ends will actually stretch those big muscles into a degree of readiness they would not have had otherwise.

Beyond that, and beyond deliberate concentration on getting shoulders and waist into your shot, you should consult your local golf pro. He or she will watch you "swat" and then help guide your body into a swing that employs more of your muscle power. When you sense how a good swing should feel at various points in that swing, you should be able to do your best.

Remember, if the full, large-muscled swing is a thing of the past for you for medical reasons, forget it. Swat away and have fun! The older you get the easier it will be to "shoot your age." At least, take that Positive Mental Attitude to the golf course with you. You may remain a "swatter," but you'll be good company.

Chapter 5

Slicing, hooking, shanking

MISTAKE

Slicing

On the downswing, the club moves outside the intended line of flight of the ball, cutting across it. This generally causes a slice, with the ball curving from the left to the right. The trouble usually starts with the shoulders pointing somewhat to the right rather than approximately at the target area. Statistically, *most* bad golf shots slice off to the right. Much of the difficulty lies in cutting across the ball with the club face.

CORRECTION

Practice swinging with the club moving from the inside to the outside in its path from your backswing toward the ball. This involves moving the arms slightly closer to the body than they were when you committed the cutting-across error.

In setting up for your shot, aim your shoulders at your target. An old Scottish instructor has his students imagine they are standing on one railroad track with the ball on the other. "Now just hit the ball down the track," he says, "and try nae to fall off the other."

If the basic target area is too far away, pick an intermediate spot that's lined up en route to where you want the ball to go.

There is some difference of opinion among pros as to whether the shoulders should absolutely aim at the target. This is something you'll have to work out in practice through trial and error. Most pros agree that the club face should point to the target, and the body should take whatever position is necessary to accomplish this.

MISTAKE

Hooking

Golf pros like to joke that any new golfer can slice the ball but only an experienced golfer can develop a hook (also known as a pull, or a draw). In a hook, the ball is pulled, or drawn, from the right to the left, the opposite of the classic and more common slice. At the moment of impact, the club angles to the left.

Hooks come from counterclockwise spin imparted to the ball by the club face at the moment of impact. The swing causing a hook usually starts inside the intended line of flight of the ball, cuts outside the line as it hits the ball, and then arcs back to the inside.

A line drawn from right toe to left toe in the slicing stance would intersect with a straight line drawn from the ball to the target—unlike railroad tracks.

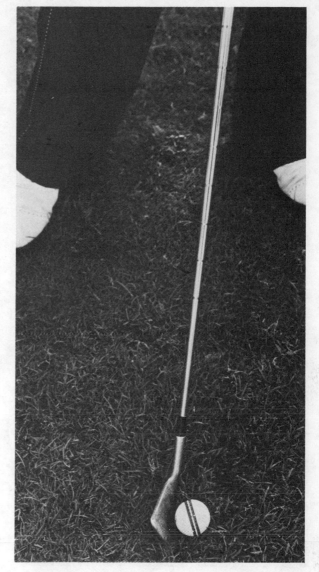

CORRECTION

Correcting the hook involves getting the club face to strike the ball squarely, with the club face and ball both aiming at the target. Working backward from this desired position, the swing must be squared up so that it doesn't go from the inside to the outside but rather makes a smooth, dead-ahead pathway. Try letting your left foot "open," or point, somewhat to the left, and practice changing foot positions until you get the uncorrected hook out of your game.

If for some reason—say, an obstacle—you want to *use* the hook, as pros do, all you have to do is consolidate your mistakes! Aspire to the inside-to-outside swing to put counterclockwise English on the ball, and line up for the shot with a somewhat "closed" stance, that is, your left foot angled in toward the intended flight path of the ball and back a couple of inches. To continue the railroad track simile, you should be standing on a track that, some place down the line, will intersect with the track of the ball.

Work on controlling the way the club face strikes the ball and you'll be able to hook, pull or draw, at will.

MISTAKE

Shanking

The common mistake of shanking—hitting the ball toward the back of the club face (at the hozel)—usually begins with too much of the body's weight on the toes. This causes the club head to move from the outside to the inside in the swing. Such cutting across the ball, or worse, can send it off erratically. Shanking also comes from shoving the right hand forward or from trying to dig a divot by hitting behind the ball with the 1, 2, or 3 iron. Shanking occurs mostly with the long irons, which seem to give golfers the most trouble.

CORRECTION

Starting with the mental picture of standing on one railroad track and setting up to swing at a ball placed on the other, the ideal antishank golf swing would have the club head move toward the ball from a slightly inside position and strike the ball at the very moment the club face is in line with the target. In this example, the club head curves back, away from the track the ball is on.

If you are teeing up for a long iron shot and are having shanking problems, tee the ball up as high as you can. However, the only long-term solution for shanking is to develop a coordinated, well-grooved swing.

Arnold Palmer recommends as an antishanking drill that you toss golf balls forward with an underhand, softball pitching motion. He wants you to feel the naturalness of the arm swing and then apply it to your golf swing. Remember to keep the right arm relaxed. Think positively and you will defeat shanking.

Chapter 6
Near the green

MISTAKE

Scooping on pitch shots

On short iron chip shots—pitch shots—accomplished mostly with the arms and hands and a minimum of body power, a common mistake is permitting the left hand to collapse and letting the right hand dominate the stroke. Usually, in this mistake the right wrist "breaks" along with the left, and the combination scoops the ball into the air—or worse.

CORRECTION

Head and body should remain relatively still in the short chip shot. Concentrate on keeping the wrists of both hands relatively steady. Too much body in this shot will cause you to hit the ball too high, so use your practice time on those arms, especially the wrists. Aim at targets from various distances away—a few feet off the green to fifty yards. The thing to strive for is consistency. When you can chip five out of ten of these arm and wrist shots into a ten-foot target area, move on to something requiring more "body" in the shot lest you forget how to use it.

65

MISTAKE

Losing your chips

The short shots in golf—those from just off the green—are the toughest to make for most golfers. From just a few feet off the green, they tend to blast away and overshoot, to "baby" the ball, or otherwise to choke up and lose their chips, if not their marbles. Some of the worst chipping faults involve lining up improperly and then trying to get back on target by using the wrists. The most common chipping fault is caused by the right hand trying to take over the shot, which makes the ball go to the left.

66

CORRECTION

The chip shot is one of golf's beautiful sights when executed properly. Whether accomplished with a "Texas wedge," the putter, from a yard off the green or from ten or fifteen yards out and down a slope, the sight of a well-hit chip flying holeward is always a thrill—unless your opponent is doing it. It is profitable for the average golfer to work hard on chipping practice because chipping can be very forgiving and get you closer to the hole than you probably deserve to be.

The chip should be thought of as a long putt. If you have a longish chip shot to accomplish, aim for a target area some place on the green, and gauge the ball's roll from that point to the hole. In other words, don't chip exactly to the flag! Aim short and let the ball roll the rest of the way. Aiming the club head is no different than in putting. Keep the face going straight through the ball to the target at the speed that practice has told you will do the job.

In setting up for the shot, concentrate on good aiming position and on using your wrists and arms more than your body. Generally, the ball is played from midway between your legs, with feet fairly close together. You want a low trajectory. Weight should rest slightly more on the left foot than the right, even though body motion is minimal on the chip.

Chapter 7
Playing the terrain

MISTAKE

Making the rough rougher than it is

When your ball lands in the rough and is playable but encumbered by grass, it is generally a mistake to attempt to hit it out with an iron. The iron will bunch up the grass on the ball, which is known as a "closing" effect, making the club turn to the left and thus throwing the "recovery" shot off. Often when hit with an iron, the ball will stagger out of the brush as a "flier," without any spin or much control.

CORRECTION

The number 4 wood is beautifully equipped to plough through entangling grass and hit the ball squarely toward the target. Furthermore, on long fairways, the 4 wood will give you good distance and, if you practice with it, accuracy. If you experience some difficulty in lofting shots with the 4 wood, try moving your stance so that the ball is an inch off the inside of your left heel.

The 4 wood is one of the most useful clubs in the professional's bag—and it should be in yours, too. If you're having trouble with your driver, alternate it with your number 4 wood. You might lose a few yards in distance, but accuracy should make up for this. A few good 4-wood drives will help you get your swing back in groove for your driver.

MISTAKE

Sloping

There are four basic slope troubles that can cause you woe: uphill, with the ball above foot level; downhill, with ball below foot level; sidehill, with ball below foot level; sidehill, with ball above foot level. The most common difficulty is in the uphill lie, where the tendency is to let the lie of the ball and the land push you back so that you "fall away" from the shot and lose such balance as you might have. Loss of balance often comes from an attempt to make this shot as if it were a normal flatland short iron stroke with normal backswing. Falling back, needless to say, will work against your accuracy.

CORRECTION

To play from the basic uphill lie with ball above right foot level, move your hands a couple of inches down the shaft of the club. Try to keep your weight leaning forward without leaning too heavily on your knees for support. Aim your iron somewhat to the right of the target to compensate for the hill. Aim for a spot on the fairway ahead of you or on the green. Use a shoulder-high backswing. A wedge or short iron will do you the most good here.

When the ball is below your back foot level, hit it from a little farther back in your stance. Aim your short iron somewhat to the left of your target. The ball should fly lower than from an uphill lie.

When you're stuck on the side of a hill with the ball above foot level, an average short iron recovery shot will tend to fly to the left, so aim a bit to the right. When the ball is lying sidehill below foot level, stand closer to it and aim to the left of the target. If you have body trouble in your swing, these are fine shots to practice because their heaviest demand is on the hands and arms.

Chapter 8
Traps

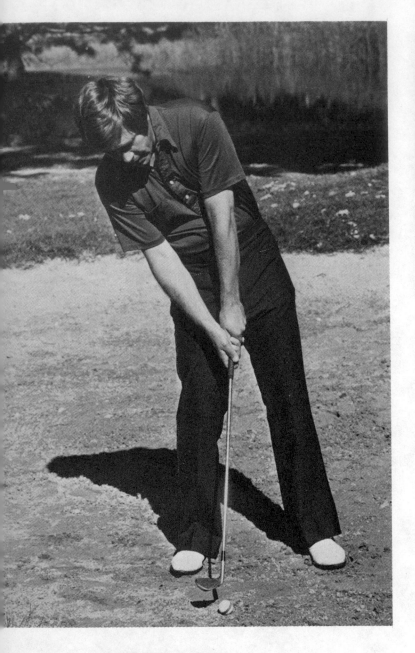

MISTAKE

Getting trapped

Next to having your ball land in a trap, the worst thing is to flail away in an effort to get out of it. There is a tendency for players when trapped to choke up a bit mentally and panic. This can destroy an ordinarily good or even fair swing. If the trap is slightly uphill, it is especially bad to let your weight fall on the back, or right, foot. This will cause the swing to break downward on contact, and you probably will top the ball.

Hitting this uphill sand lie as if it were a level shot on the fairway is also a mistake that probably will roll the shot to the lip of the trap and then back down. Using a closed stance—left foot parallel to right in relation to the flight of the ball—will also add to your troubles.

CORRECTION

To hit uphill in sand for a relatively short approach, you should hit the sand, not the ball! Aim a couple of inches behind the ball and use an open stance—left foot pulled back a couple of inches. This helps your somewhat restricted swing and also should help you keep your balance as you follow through. On downhill lies you should practice hitting a bit farther behind the ball than on uphill lies. (This accounts for some of those great "explo-sions" you see on TV trap shots.)

The longer the shot from the trap, the closer your club face must hit to the ball. This is one of those golf shots that demands more of the arms than of the entire body, although the knees should flex gently on the swing. When the sand in the trap is hard, the ball should be played off the forward edge of the front foot. You can align it safely with your left instep.

Chapter 9
Wind

MISTAKE

Wind troubles

When you are driving downwind (wind at your back) there is a tendency by many golfers to tee the ball too low and play it from too near the middle of their stance. They don't make any kind of adjustment for the carrying power of the wind. The longer the shot, the more influence the wind will have on it.

If the ball is hit well, the wind will carry it past your aiming point. If the ball is hit poorly but with some loft, it will go off even farther because of the wind.

CORRECTION

When shooting from the tee with the wind behind you, tee the ball up as high as you can, and move the ball a few inches forward from where you would ordinarily (no wind) strike it. This correction often results in hitting the ball higher into the air, which permits you to use the wind's power to help move your ball toward its target.

Obviously, when confronted with the opposite situation—hitting into the wind—you should correct your stroke, if it needs correction, by teeing the ball closer to the ground and moving it back a few inches before swinging.

Chapter 10

Obstacles and other woes

MISTAKE

Striking high obstacle

Between nature and the modern golf course architect, many a tree stands in the way of a golfer and his green. Hitting a tree rather than clearing it can put a severe crimp in your score and be otherwise embarrassing.

Hitting too low is generally the result of setting up so that the ball is too far back in the stance—off the right heel, as in the photo. This invariably results in a flat-footed swing and an improper weight transfer from rear to front foot.

The ball will skitter low, hardly high enough to clear the tree.

CORRECTION

The feet should be turned slightly to the left of the target. The ball should be played somewhat more off the left foot with your wedge or 9 iron. This, coupled with a smooth swing and better weight transfer, will create a descending motion and force the ball into the air after impact.

In practice, this shot is one of the easi-est to perfect. The wedge and other short irons should be tried experimentally until you feel confident that you can clear an imaginary tree on the practice range.

Setting up with the ball well back and remaining mindful of good weight transfer are the secrets to getting the ball up high enough to suit your real or imagined situation.

85

MISTAKE

Playing a sunken ball

If your ball lands in a puddle or in low water at the edge of a water hazard, don't try to blast it out from under water. You will invariably hit the laws of physics and refraction before you hit the ball.

CORRECTION

If your ball is submerged, take your one stroke penalty and drop the ball over your shoulder on the closest dry land.

If you can see more than half of your ball above the surface of the water, try a 5 iron, setting up with the ball off your left heel. Swing down and hard, a little behind the ball, as in a sandtrap shot.

Don't practice this excessively unless you don't care about your clothing. Wipe your clubs carefully after a submarine venture.

MISTAKE

Obstacle to obstacle shots

Trying to hit the ball low to keep it under a protruding branch, the golfer makes his shot with his weight on his back foot. This only throws the ball high into the air without power or accuracy and increases your chances of hitting the tree. It is in pressure situations such as this that the fundamentals are most often breached.

CORRECTION

With proper weight shift from back foot to front, even an obstacle becomes manageable. The tendency to "sky" the ball disappears with the proper body movement. A low trajectory is obviously what this shot demands. In practicing your irons, try using your body shift to keep a series of practice shots low. The other parts of your game will fall into place once you learn to get that weight from the back to the front foot as you strike the ball.

Chapter 11
Putting

MISTAKE

Not reading the putting green

One of the nation's top groundskeepers, Oak Park's Al Fierst, says, "It really hurts me when I see golfers on the green take a quick look at their ball, a glance at the flag, and then putt—usually missing by long yards." Teaching pros know what he means.

Fierst's pride in his rolling greens is piqued by golfers who make the mistake of not studying the way the grass lies and the rolls and undulations of a beautifully kept green.

Most putting errors are made while putting downhill. Generally, the ball is hit too hard, without taking gravity into account. That kind of error will roll your putt far past the hole. Not reading the roll of the green will throw it off sideways in one direction or another.

This golfer is shown mistakenly putting "straight." He is aiming directly at the cup, without acknowledging the roll of the green.

92

CORRECTION

Gently rolling greens are generally the most beautiful—and most treacherous—to the inexperienced putter. The golfer should squat down and take note of how the green rolls in relation to his ball.

On a cup-like green, such as this one, the ball must be stroked on an arc that carries it several feet off of a straight line but into the cup. Judging speed and distance "on the curve" takes much practice.

The ideal arc for making this 20-footer down a curved green is shown by placing a succession of balls along the path this putt must travel.

MISTAKE

Poor eye position for putting

No area of golf gives more trouble than putting or has more theories surrounding it. The simple art of hitting the ball those last few feet along the green and into the hole escapes most golfers from the very beginning because of a simple, basic fault—the eyes sight the ball from an angle. With the eyes focused somewhat behind the ball, looking down at it, it is difficult to judge (*consistently*—the key word to improving your golf) where and how hard to tap the ball.

Given the many variables of the putting situation—green level, grass condition, etc.—adding poor eye position when looking down at the ball contributes to poor putting.

94

CORRECTION

Unless you have a great natural eye, use your putter as a plumb bob, and center your eyes precisely over the ball. With your eyes in position directly above the ball, take a comfortable stance. Let your eyes lead you!

MISTAKE

Hit or miss putting practice

Dumping a pail of balls on a golf green and whacking away at them is a poor way to learn putting. If it accomplishes anything, random practice putting will merely consolidate the errors that you and your putter bring to the green.

96

CORRECTION

Once you've established a putting stance and eye position that works for you, devote half an hour to lining up five or six balls next to each other at various positions on the green. If you have trouble with ten-footers, line up ten or twelve at that distance. Then, without rushing and taking each practice putt as a challenge, start putting. Your confidence will grow, and the next time you have to putt in a match, you will be prepared to do your very best at whatever distance you are challenged.

Chapter 12
Mental golf

MISTAKE

Not visualizing your shot

Most teaching professionals, especially those who are on the pro tour, agree that as many as 75 percent of all golf errors are mental. In golf (as in most sports) it is a mistake not to use your "inner game"—your thinking—to improve your shots.

A negative mental attitude ("I can't possibly make that shot") or building up a mental specter of "a miss"—actually "seeing" the ball go into the lip of the bank for a bogie or worse—helps make the instant bad dream come true. Usually, the head full of negatives tends to freeze up and stiffen the parts of the body you need for your shot.

100

CORRECTION

Think positively! Imagine that you are going to *make* that shot or come darn close! Whether you call it Positive Mental Attitude, inner golf, or just fantasizing, the procedure is:

1) Line up your shot.
2) Decide on the proper flight the ball must take to go where you want it to go.
3) As you prepare to hit the ball, IMAGINE the ball describing the flight pattern you have visualized, right to the hole!
4) EXPECT the ball to follow your mental plan for it.

This is a good way to keep business and other worries from intruding on the concentration it takes to make a good golf shot.

Carrying Positive Mental Attitude a step further, sports therapist Karen L. Reischel, while on the faculty of the University of Washington, made studies on successes and failures in six sports. She concluded: "Those athletes who imagined themselves as winners—could actually see themselves being congratulated after a shot or match—in fact were nearly 40 percent more effective than non-visualizing opponents of otherwise equal ability."

MISTAKE

Not concentrating

Golf is, of course, a fun game that must be taken seriously to be enjoyed. Practice is the only route to achievement. It is, therefore, a mistake to reduce practice sessions to conversation and joke time. Mental concentration suffers when practice sessions deteriorate, willy-nilly, into hit-or-miss drills.

CORRECTION

It's a good idea to practice all departments of golf, at least for a little while, before playing a game. Systematic attention must be paid to woods, irons, and, especially, putting.

One of the top money-winning golfers in the country, Andy Bean, is shown concentrating on his putting before the U.S. Western Open. Bean says, "Most beginners take too much backswing on putting. This accelerates the ball too much. I accelerate just as I hit, perhaps a bit afterward." This is what he is concentrating on in this session.

The ability to concentrate has kept Arnold Palmer in the ranks of the all-time greats for 15 years. Here, in the same tournament for which Bean was preparing, Palmer's concentration on the game, his lie, and his next shot seem to permeate and dominate the scene. This concentration and ability to focus—a learned skill, because in the beginning Palmer used to look up at airplanes—is one of the reasons he has "charged" time and again to win a tournament in the final few holes.

Here are just a few of the practice balls that the pros in the Western Open used on only one morning of practice! So practice correcting your mistakes. In any case, practice!

Index